Queen Victoria

Dereen Taylor

First published in 2007 by Wayland
Copyright © Wayland 2007

Wayland
338 Euston Road
London NW1 3BH

Wayland Australia
Level 17/207 Kent Street
Sydney, NSW 2000

Editor: Victoria Brooker
Designer: Jane Stanley

Taylor, Dereen
  Who was Queen Victoria?
  1. Victoria, Queen of Great Britain, 1819-1901 - Juvenile
  literature 2. Great Britain - Kings and rulers - Biography
  - Juvenile literature 3. Great Britain - History -
  Victoria, 1837-1901 - Juvenile literature
  I. Title
  941'.081'092
ISBN 978 0 7502 5193 8

Printed in China
Wayland is a division of Hachette Children's Books, an Hachette Livre UK Company.

For permission to reproduce the following pictures, the author and publisher would like
to thank: Bettmann/Corbis: 18; Stefan Bianchetti/Corbis: 19; City Museums & Art
Gallery, Plymouth, Devon, UK/Bridgeman Art Library, London: 20; Mary Evans Picture
Library: 7, 12, 21; Getty Images (Hulton Archive): 6, 13, 16, 17; Private Collection/
Bridgeman Art Library, London: 11 Private Collection/©Archives Charmet/Bridgeman
Art Library: 4, Cover; Private Collection/Photo©Christie's Images/Bridgeman Art
Library, London: 8; Private Collection/©Dreweatt Neate Fine Art Auctioneers, Newbury,
Berks, UK/Bridgeman Art Library, London: 9; Private Collection/©Look and Learn/
Bridgeman Art Library, London: 14; Topham Picturepoint/TopFoto: 5; Victoria & Albert
Museum, London/Sally Chappell/The Art Archive: 10; Laurie Platt Winfrey/The Art
Archive: 15

Contents

Words in **bold** can be found in the glossary.

Who was Queen Victoria?

Queen Victoria ruled over Britain and the **British Empire** from 1837 to 1901. She was Queen for 64 years. This was the longest **reign** of any British king or queen.

This portrait of Queen Victoria was painted in 1887.

This photograph is of a middle-class Victorian family at home. It was taken towards the end of Victoria's reign in 1889.

We call people who lived at that time Victorians. The Victorians liked the royal family and crowds came to see Queen Victoria wherever she went.

Places to Visit

Buckingham Palace. Queen Victoria was the first British **monarch** to live there. Today it is the London home of Queen Elizabeth II.

Victoria's childhood

Queen Victoria was born in 1819. She was the only child of Prince Edward and his German wife, Princess Victoria.

Victoria's mother called her daughter by a special name, 'Drina', when the two of them were together.

Victoria's father died when she was a baby. She grew up in Kensington Palace in London with her mother.

Victoria didn't go to school with other children. Instead, she was taught German, French, history and maths at home. The young Victoria enjoyed singing and painting.

As a girl Victoria had lessons on her own with her teacher.

Places to Visit

Kensington Palace, London. There is a large statue of Queen Victoria in front of the palace. It was sculpted by Victoria's daughter, Princess Louise, to celebrate Queen Victoria's Golden Jubilee in 1887.

Heir to the throne

Victoria's uncle, King William IV, had no children. This meant Victoria was **heir** to the British throne. When William IV died in 1837, Victoria became Queen of Great Britain and Ireland. She was just eighteen years old.

This portrait shows Queen Victoria in her **coronation** robes. She is about to wear the royal crown for the first time.

Her coronation was a year later at Westminster Abbey. Thousands of coronation souvenirs were sold to celebrate this important event.

The British people rushed out to buy coronation souvenirs. This was a way of showing their support for the young Queen.

Victoria and Albert

In 1840, when Victoria was 21, she married Prince Albert. He was her German cousin. Victoria listened to Albert's advice and he helped her do her job as Queen.

Victoria and Albert were very happily married and enjoyed spending time together.

In 1851 Prince Albert organised the Crystal Palace Exhibition. This was a huge fair that showed off the best **inventions** from around the world.

The Crystal Palace Exhibition in 1851 showed the world the achievements of the **British Empire**.

Sons and daughters

Queen Victoria and Prince Albert had a happy life together. They had nine children — four sons and five daughters. They were called Victoria, Albert Edward, Alice, Alfred, Helena, Louise, Arthur, Leopold and Beatrice.

This family photograph of Queen Victoria and Prince Albert with their children was taken in about 1860.

Through the marriages of her children and grandchildren, Queen Victoria was related to many royal families in Europe. She was sometimes known as 'The Grandmother of Europe'.

Victoria and Albert made the German custom of Christmas trees popular in Britain.

Victorian inventions

Queen Victoria's **reign** also saw the arrival of many important **inventions**. The **engineer** Isambard Kingdom Brunel built railway bridges and tunnels, which are still used today. The first car powered by petrol instead of steam went on sale to the public in 1884.

Places to Visit

You can see many Victorian inventions at the Science Museum in London.

Queen Victoria made her first train journey on a steam train like this.

In 1876, the Scottish inventor Alexander Graham Bell invented the first telephone. In 1878, Queen Victoria used a telephone for the first time at Osborne House.

This photograph of Alexander Graham Bell shows him using his 'electrical speech machine'. We now call this invention the telephone.

Victoria in mourning

Queen Victoria's much loved husband Albert died from **typhoid** in 1861. Victoria was heartbroken and was not seen in public for over ten years.

After Albert's death, Queen Victoria always wore black to show how much she missed her husband.

She spent most of her time at Balmoral Castle in Scotland. This made Victoria unpopular with the Victorians. They wanted her to act like their Queen again.

IT'S TRUE!

After Albert's death, Victoria had a smaller crown made that sat on top of the veil she always wore.

Prince Albert had bought Balmoral Castle as a gift for the Queen in 1852.

The British Empire

During the **reign** of Queen Victoria, Britain ruled countries all over the world. These countries belonged to the **British Empire**.

This cartoon appeared in a newspaper in 1876. It shows the Prime Minister, Benjamin Disraeli, making Queen Victoria Empress of India.

Britain was becoming richer and more successful. The countries in the Empire provided Britain with food and **materials** such as cotton and rubber. British factories turned these materials into **goods** that were sold all over the world.

It was a long, hard day for these women working in a cotton factory in Derby.

Queen Victoria's death

Queen Victoria was seen again in public in 1887, for her Golden Jubilee. She had been Queen for 50 years.

This cup and saucer were made to celebrate the Queen's Golden Jubilee in 1887.

On 22 June 1897 it was the Queen's Diamond Jubilee. People marched through London to give thanks for Victoria's sixty years as Queen.

Queen Victoria died
at Osborne House in 1901.
For most people, Victoria
had been a popular Queen
and the only **monarch**
they had ever known.

Places to Visit

St George's Chapel,
Windsor Castle is where
Queen Victoria's funeral
was held in 1901. Queen
Victoria and Prince Albert
are both buried there.

This portrait
shows the
coffin of
Queen Victoria
being guarded
by soldiers at
Osborne
House on the
Isle of Wight.

Timeline

1819 Princess Alexandrina Victoria is born on 24 May

1837 Victoria becomes Queen on 20 June

1838 Queen Victoria's coronation at Westminster Abbey on 28 June

1840 Queen Victoria marries Prince Albert on 10 February

1851 Great Exhibition at Crystal Palace

1852 Prince Albert buys Balmoral Castle in Scotland for Queen Victoria

1861 Prince Albert dies on 14 December
       Queen Victoria goes into mourning

1876 Queen Victoria becomes Empress of India
       Scottish inventor Alexander Graham Bell invents the first telephone

1887 Queen Victoria's Golden Jubilee celebrating fifty years
       on the throne

1897 Queen Victoria's Diamond Jubilee celebrating sixty years
       on the throne

1901 Queen Victoria dies at Osborne House on 22 January
       Queen Victoria's eldest son becomes King Edward VII

Glossary

British Empire countries around the world under the rule of the British monarch

coronation the ceremony held when a new monarch is crowned king or queen

crowned to crown somebody is to give them the royal crown and make them king or queen of a country

engineer someone who makes machines, or plans the building of roads and bridges

goods things that can be bought and sold

heir someone who inherits a role or estate from another

invention a new object that has been created

materials anything solid that can be used to make something else. Cotton, rubber and wood are all materials

monarch another word for a king or queen

reign the period during which a king or queen rules

typhoid a serious infection that is caught from dirty food or water

Further information

Books

The Life and World of Queen Victoria by Brian Williams
(Heinemann Library, 2002)

Famous People, Famous Lives: Queen Victoria by Harriet Castor
(Franklin Watts, 2002)

Websites

http://www.bbc.co.uk/history/historic_figures/victoria_queen.shtml
A biography of Queen Victoria for use with teachers and parents.

http://www.bbc.co.uk/schools/victorians/
BBC schools website explores the life of children in Victorian times.

Index